Unstoppable Negotiating: How To Wrap Up A Negotiation And Get The Deal That You Want, How To Develop The Skill Of Closing In Order To Get The Best Possible Outcome From A Negotiation

Copyright 2017 by Jim Anderson

Kindle Edition

Published by

Blue Elephant Consulting

Tampa, Florida

All rights reserved. No part of this book may be reproduced of transmitted in any form or by any means, electronic or mechanical, including photocopying, recording or by any information storage and retrieval system without written permission of the publisher, except for inclusion of brief quotations in a review.

Printed in the United States of America

Library of Congress Control Number: 2018938607

ISBN-13: 978-1986676403

ISBN-10: 1986676404

Recent Books By The Author

Product Management

Manage Your Customers, Manage Your Product: Techniques For Product Managers To Better Understand What Their Customers Really Want

Managing Your Product Manager Career: How Product Managers Can Find And Succeed In The Right Job

Public Speaking

How To Get Ready To Give The Perfect Speech: What Tools To Use To Create Your Next Speech So That Your Message Will Be Remembered Forever!

Creating Speeches That Work: How To Create A Speech That Will Make Your Message Be Remembered Forever!

CIO Skills

How CIOs Can Take Their Career To The Next Level: How CIOs Can Work With The Entire Company In Order To Be Successful

How CIOs Can Bring Business And IT Together: How CIOs Can Use Their Technical Skills To Help Their Company Solve Real-World Business Problems

IT Manager Skills

Understanding What Leadership Means For IT Managers: Tips And Techniques That IT Managers Can Use In Order To Develop Leadership Skills

How IT Managers Can Use New Technology To Meet Today's IT Challenges: Technologies That IT Managers Can Use In Order to Make Their Teams More Productive

Negotiating

The Art Of Packaging A Negotiation: How To Develop The Skill Of Assembling Potential Trades In Order To Get The Best Possible Outcome

Getting What You Want In A Negotiation By Learning How To Signal: How To Develop The Skill Of Effective Signaling In A Negotiation In Order To Get The Best Possible Outcome

Miscellaneous

How To Heal A Broken Leg – Fast!: Understanding how to deal with a broken leg in order to start walking again quickly

How Software Defined Networking (SDN) Is Going To Change Your World Forever: The Revolution In Network Design And How It Affects

Note: See a complete list of books by Dr. Jim Anderson at the back of this book.

Acknowledgements

Any book like this one is the result of years of real-world work experience. In my over 25 years of working for 7 different firms, I have met countless fantastic people and I've been mentored by some truly exceptional ones. Although I've probably forgotten some of the people who made me the person that I am today, here is my attempt to finally give them the recognition that they so truly deserve:

- Thomas P. Anderson
- Art Puett
- Bobbi Marshall
- Bob Boggs

Dr. Jim Anderson

This book is dedicated to my family: Lori, Maddie, Nick, and Ben. None of this would have been possible without their constant love and support.

Thanks for always believing in me and providing me with the strength to always be willing to go out there and be my best for you.

Table Of Contents

WALK AWAY WITH THE DEAL THAT YOU WANTED 7

ABOUT THE AUTHOR 9

CHAPTER 1: REAL WORLD SALES NEGOTIATIONS: CLEAR CHANNEL TAKES IT TO THE BRINK 14

CHAPTER 2: QUICK CLOSE NEGOTIATING: 4 WAYS TO GET THERE FASTER 18

CHAPTER 3: WHAT DOES "TAKE IT OR LEAVE IT" MEAN IN A SALES NEGOTIATION? 22

CHAPTER 4: GOING UP? HOW SALES NEGOTIATORS DEAL WITH ESCALATION 26

CHAPTER 5: WHY A MISSING PERSON MAY BE A NEGOTIATOR'S BEST FRIEND 30

CHAPTER 6: SALES NEGOTIATORS ASK "DO YOU SEE WHAT I SEE..."? 34

CHAPTER 7: THE ULTIMATE SALES NEGOTIATING GOAL: A SHARED VISION 37

CHAPTER 8: I'VE MET THE NEGOTIATING DEVIL AND HE LIVES IN THE DETAILS 41

CHAPTER 9: WHEN "YES" MEANS "NO" AND WHAT TO DO ABOUT IT 45

CHAPTER 10: NEGOTIATORS KNOW HOW TO GET A DEAL INTO SHAPE 49

CHAPTER 11: SUCCESSFUL NEGOTIATORS KNOW WHAT MONEY LOOKS LIKE 53

CHAPTER 12: WHEN IS IT TIME TO BRING IN THE MEDIATOR? ..57

Walk Away With The Deal That You Wanted

All negotiations have to come to a close. When your next negotiation reaches this stage, you want to make sure that you are going to be able to walk away with the best deal possible. In order to make this happen, it's going to be what you've done during the negotiations that will determine what your outcome is.

Some people believe that negotiations have to take a long time and that they can drag on forever. However, it turns out that a skilled negotiator can cause a negotiation to wrap up in record time. There may be times with the other side tells you to "take it or leave it". You need to understand what they are really saying and how to react. During a negotiation, the other side may decide that they need to bring in more senior people in order to get what they want. You'll need to understand how to deal with this in order to ensure that you'll get the deal that you want.

We often believe that it's who we bring to the negotiating table that will determine the deal that we get. However, in some cases it's really who is not there that will control the outcome. Ever negotiation is not the same. The way that you look at a negotiation may not be the same way that the other side is looking at it. One of the best ways to get what you want is to make it what the other side wants by developing a shared vision that both of you can work towards.

In every negotiation, there are many different moving parts. Your job as a negotiator is to keep track of everything that is going on because it's the details that will control the type of deal that you'll get. Remember that just because the other side has agreed to something does not mean that they really want it. They may change their mind later on. Almost every negotiation deals with money in some fashion and this means that negotiators need to understand what money looks like in all of its different forms. We can't always wrap up a negotiation by ourselves. Sometimes we're going to have to bring in a mediator to get the deal that we want.

For more information on what it takes to be a great negotiator, check out my blog, The Accidental Negotiator, at:

www.TheAccidentalNegotiator.com

Good luck!

- Dr. Jim Anderson

About The Author

I must confess that I never set out to be a negotiator. When I went to school, I studied Computer Science and thought that I'd get a nice job programming and that would be that. Well, at least part of that plan worked out!

My first job was working for Boeing on their F/A-18 fighter jet program. I spent my days programming fighter jet software in assembly language and I loved it. The U.S. government decided to save some money and went looking for other countries to sell this plane to. This put me into an unfamiliar role: I started to negotiate with foreign military officials and I ended up having to participate in the negotiations for large international deals.

Time moved on and so did I. I found myself working for Siemens, the big German telecommunications company. They were making phone switches and selling them to the seven U.S. phone companies. The problem was that the switches were too complicated. When it came time to negotiate a deal with the customer, the sales teams struggled to create an effective negotiating strategy. I was called in to bridge the world between the product functionality and the business impacts as they related to the negotiations.

I've spent over 25 years working as a negotiator for both big companies and startups. This has given me an opportunity to learn what it takes to both plan and execute negotiations of all sizes. When it comes to negotiations, I've pretty much been there, done that.

I now live in Tampa Florida where I spend my time managing my consulting business, Blue Elephant Consulting, teaching college courses at the University of South Florida, and traveling to work with companies like yours to share the knowledge that I have about how to prepare for and execute successful negotiations.

I'm always available to answer questions and I can be reached at:

Dr. Jim Anderson
Blue Elephant Consulting
Email: jim@BlueElephantConsulting.com
Facebook: http://goo.gl/1TVoK
Web: **www.BlueElephantConsulting.com**

**"Unforgettable communication skills that will
set your ideas free..."**

Create An Effective Negotiating Team At Your Company!

Dr. Jim Anderson is available to provide training and coaching on the topics that are the most important to people who have to negotiate: how can my team effectively prepare for and execute a successful negotiation that will get us what we both want and need?

Dr. Anderson believes that in order to both learn and remember what he says, audiences need to laugh. Each one of his speeches is full of fun and humor so that what he says "sticks" with everyone.

Dr. Anderson's Negotiating Training Includes:

1. How to plan for a negotiation: what information do you need and where can you find it?

2. What's the best way to explore how a deal can be created during a negotiation?

3. How can you bring a negotiation to a close without giving in to the other side?

Dr. Jim Anderson works with over 100 customers per year. To invite Dr. Anderson to work with you, contact him at:

Phone: 813-418-6970 or
Email: jim@BlueElephantConsulting.com

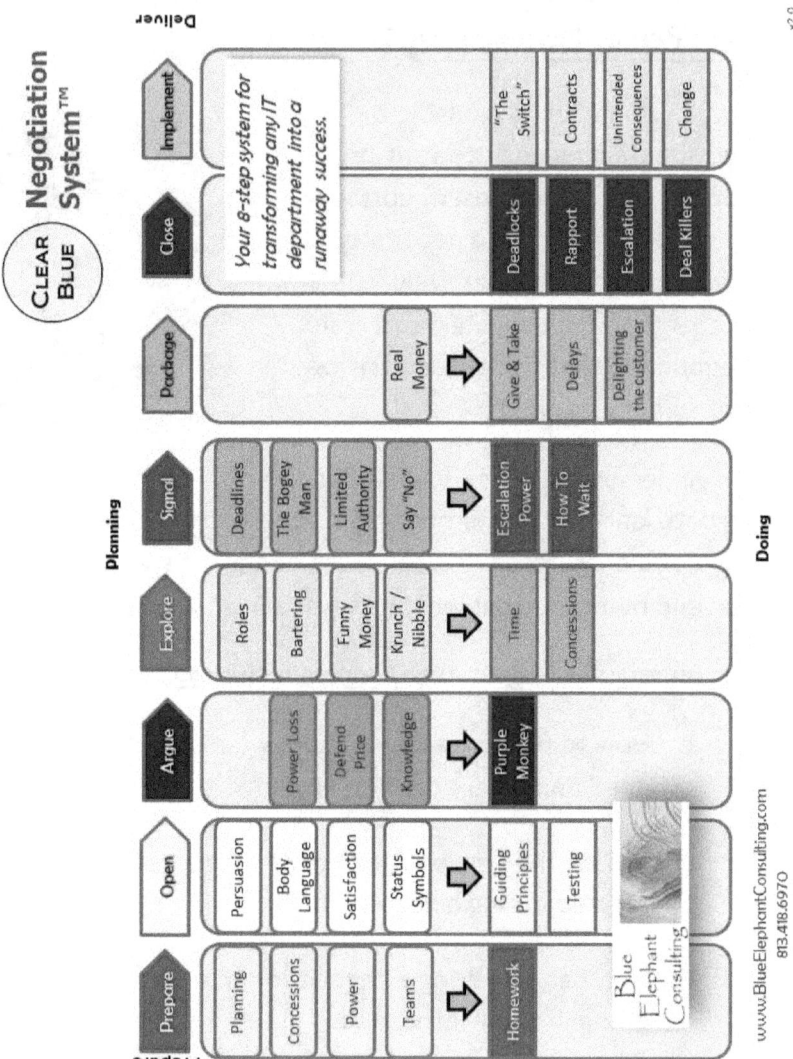

The **Clear Blue Negotiation System™** has been created to provide negotiators with a clear roadmap for how to manage a successful negotiation. This system shows negotiators what needs to be done and in what order to do it.

Chapter 1

Real World Sales Negotiations: Clear Channel Takes It To The Brink

Chapter 1: Real World Sales Negotiations: Clear Channel Takes It To The Brink

It's all too easy to get caught up in the theory of negotiating and sometimes we forget to take the time to look around us and **see other deals that are being made** — and learn from them. If we needed a recent deal to teach us a lesson, the $20 billion dollar Clear Channel private equity buy-out would be a good example — because it almost didn't happen!

The Background Of The Clear Channel Deal

Once upon a time Clear Channel was a high-flying communications company (in the 1990's). Their stock traded at north of **$100 per share**. That was then, this is now — their stock has been in the dumpster for a while now and was trading in the low $30's.

The company decided that what needed to be done is that they needed to **go private**. No problem with that decision, it's just that it takes a whole lotta money to buy up all of those outstanding shares of stock.

This is where various private equity firms and **six different Wall Street banks** came in. A deal was struck to buy the company for $24.4 billion.

A Problem Arises

When somebody is getting ready to pay a lot of money for your company, the last thing in the world that you want to have happen is to start having **legal problems**. That, of course, is exactly what happened: Clear Channel got sued at the same time in two different states.

This of course messed with the **value of the company** and that made all of the bankers very mad — it was looking like they had agreed to pay too much for the company.

Things got so bad that when Clear Channel's executives placed calls to the six bankers on the deal, only one of them called back. One of the reasons that the others didn't call back was that they were afraid that the conversation could get introduced into court proceedings. People who worked on the deal said that the **hatred** (their word, not mine) got so bad that it was almost palpable.

Negotiation Comes To The Rescue

So how did Clear Channel and the bankers resolve their impasse? **Negotiation of course** (this blog is called The Accidental Negotiator after all!). How did they do this?

- **Egos Away!:** Everyone involved took a step back and put their egos away for at least awhile (we are after all talking about Wall Street folks here).

- **2nd Look:** Next they took a second look at the deal that was on the table and started to get clinical about how they were going to go about doing the financing.

- **Mistrust:** The banks had been reading the body language of the private-equity firms as saying that they didn't want to do a deal anymore (at least at the price that had been agreed to originally).

- **Red Herrings:** The banks started to make demands regarding the length of time that Clear Channel would be allowed to take a revolving loan and other items that had nothing to do with the price of the deal. These were all just a smoke screen.

In the end, **it all got negotiated**. The private-equity firms got the revolving credit from the banks that they believed they needed to make the company a success. The banks got a higher spread on the deal and ended up taking on less debt than they had originally signed up for.

What All Of This Means For You

Each of us ends up negotiating every day. It can be easy to get caught up in our own little world and **forget to keep our eyes open** so that we can see others who are also involved in the negotiation game. It is from them that often we can learn the most.

Clear Channel thought that they had a deal all wrapped up to sell themselves to willing buyers until **the credit crunch came along**. When the environment changed, along with a couple of lawsuits, the other partners in the deal wanted to make changes.

What started off very badly — anger and resentment were in ample supply, ended up with **a new deal getting negotiated**. What's key for us to take away from this event is that having the ability to step back from an emotional deal, focus on what's really at stake, and then find the courage to move forward is the mark of a great negotiator.

Chapter 2

Quick Close Negotiating: 4 Ways To Get There Faster

Chapter 2: Quick Close Negotiating: 4 Ways To Get There Faster

I'm pretty sure that any sales negotiator who was given a choice would always choose to **close a deal quicker** rather than slower. Sure, there are probably some masochists out there, but let's assume that everyone else would choose the quicker option. Great, now just exactly how do we go about doing this?

Bring The Backup

One way to move a deal along is to spend time before the negotiation thinking about **how you believe that it's going to unfold**. As you try to visualize how things are going to go, think through how you are going to be supporting your position at each step of the process.

This is going to bring up a good question of at each step: how are you going to give the other side of the table **that little nudge** to move in the direction that you want them to go? Once you've figured this out, you need to show up at the negotiating table prepared – you need backup.

Whatever it's going to take to convince the other side to move the way that you want them to move, that's the kind of **backup** that you want to have on your side of the table.

Shh – They Can't Say That!

The quickest way to wrap-up a sales negotiation is to make sure that the other side of the table **gets what they want**. Sounds easy enough, right? Well, maybe not. Often times the reasons that a negotiation can drag on for so long is because the other side can't tell you exactly what they want to get out of the negotiation.

It's up to you to find out what they really need. This often requires you to place yourself in their position and understand their ecosystem. There is always the possibility that they are afraid that the results of the negotiation are going to result in more work for them, or that they'll be replaced, or that they may come away looking like they didn't try hard enough to get a good deal.

Once you understand their true goals, you can steer the negotiations to meet these goals and by doing this **you may considerably shorten the whole process**.

What's Behind Door #2?

I can tell you from lots and lots of personal negotiating experience, if you're not careful you can end up **wasting a lot of time** working on negotiations that are never going to go anywhere.

That's why before you start any negotiation you need to take the time to sit down and ask yourself "**what's my next option if this just doesn't work out?**" With a little luck you won't have to use that option, but knowing what it is can help you to terminate bad negotiation sessions early on and save everyone a lot of needless pain.

Future Vision

You know how it always seems to go: you get done with a negotiation, you shake hands with the other side of the table, and then as you are in the car, on the plane, whatever, on the way home it suddenly hits you "**dang, I should have asked for …**".

While there is no way to completely prevent this from ever happening again, one thing that you can do is to take the time before you start the negotiation and **mentally picture yourself having just completed a successful deal**. Now picture yourself walking away from the table and congratulating yourself. Keep picturing it, keep picturing it – now think about what you might have missed. You'll be amazed at how many important things you'll uncover and remember to include in the main negotiations when you do this.

What All Of This Means For You

Nobody ever gets up in the morning and says to themselves, "Gosh, I hope that I get to spend all day locked in a negotiation." Since we all want to get to the end of each negotiation as quickly as possible, it sure seems like **setting the stage** to wrap things up quickly would be a good idea.

We've covered **four different ways** that you can do this. Not all of these will apply to every negotiation that you are involved in; however, generally you'll be able to use at least one.
One side benefit of becoming known as a sales negotiator who can quickly reach a deal is that **more people will want to negotiate with you**. We all seek to avoid pain, and if you are the answer to making this happen, then your negotiating popularity will soar…

Chapter 3

What Does "Take It Or Leave It" Mean In A Sales Negotiation?

Chapter 3: What Does "Take It Or Leave It" Mean In A Sales Negotiation?

The one thing that you never want to hear during a sales negotiation is the other side of the table telling you to "... take it or leave it." It sure doesn't seem as though you have any other options when they tell you this. Or do you...?

The Power Of 5 Words

Nothing can bring a negotiating session to a close quicker than having someone tell you to "take it or leave it" when it comes to the offer that they have made to you. It sure seems like this type of statement goes against everything that we've learned about negotiating: it's all about talking it out.

For some mysterious reason, these five simple words and the way that they are normally stated have an almost magical effect on every negotiator. We start to shut down when we hear them – our ability to look for other options goes away and we feel as though we are stuck with just two paths forward: accept or reject the other side's offer.

Your First Line Of Defense: Time

All too often, when we come face-to-face with the dreaded "take it or leave it" statement, we just go ahead and blurt something out (more often than not we end up saying "ok"). This is the wrong approach to take.

The next time that someone uses this line on you, do nothing, say nothing. Remember, they are taking a risk in laying this ultimatum on you and they have no idea how you are going to react. By doing (and saying) nothing, you are making them doubt themselves – did they do the wrong thing? Are you going to walk away?

Depending on where the negotiations are at and what your personal time line is, you can take this non communication tactic to the next level –you can get up and walk out. This sends a clear message to the other side – you're not happy. Keep your ears open, they may react to your silence and your movements to leave. If they start to backtrack, then you've won.

Your Second Line Of Defense: The Counteroffer

The other side has made you an offer that you really don't want. What should you do now? Taking the time needed to study it is a great first step.

Is the price that they are willing to pay too low? Are they offering to sell you too little of a product? Whatever they are offering to you as a part of their "take it or leave it" proposal, you can now adjust what you are offering to them to match their proposal.

If their price is too low, reduce the amount that you are willing to sell to them and make it match their price. If the quantity that they are willing to sell to you is too small, then reduce your price to match their quantity.

Understand Where All Of This Is Going To Lead To

Once the other side of the table has dropped the "take it or leave it" bomb, you need to realize where this negotiation is going to end up. If they really mean it, then the negotiation is probably over – unless you are willing to accept their offer.

If they don't mean it, then the ball is in your court. It's going to be up to you to push back and provide another option for both sides to negotiate.

What All Of This Means For You

No sales negotiator ever wants to hear the other side say the words "...take it or leave it." However, you will eventually hear it and that means that you've got to be ready when you do.

The most important thing that you can do when you come face-to-face with this challenge is to initially not react: don't say or do anything. Let the other side start to worry about what they've done. Getting up and leaving the negotiations is another option that you have. Finally, take the time to create a counter proposal that matches what they are willing to do. This may serve to jump-start the negotiations.

Just because the other side has made what appears to be a final proposal, you don't have to accept it as such. Remember that the ball is now in your court and what happens next is all up to you...!

Chapter 4

Going Up? How Sales Negotiators Deal With Escalation

Chapter 4: Going Up? How Sales Negotiators Deal With Escalation

Just when you think that you've got everything nailed down in a sales negotiation, you just might run into the issue of escalating authority. Sure you've reached a deal with the other side of the table, but then all of a sudden **somebody else gets involved** and it turns out that they don't like your deal. What's a sales negotiator to do?

What Is Escalating Authority?

The escalating authority tactic is a sneaky one – often you don't see it coming **until it's too late**. The way that it works is actually pretty simple. You sit down with the other side of the table and you work to hash out a deal. In the end, you both finally come up with a deal that you believe that both of you can live with.

Emotionally you believe that you are just about done with this sale and you start to think about all of the other things that you need to start to work on. That's when you get surprised. What happens is that the other side of the table comes back to you and says that **there's a problem**.

What he says is that there are **other people** in his organization who have to approve the deal that the two of you have created. He'll tell you that somebody is unwilling to approve the deal as it currently stands. They want more concessions from you in order for them to sign it.

You might be saying to yourself "I'd never give in and agree to more concessions." Well, it turns out that a lot of us actually do give in and do end up **making more concessions** – that's why this technique is so effective.

How Can You Make Escalating Authority Work For You?

We all think the same thing when we bump into a powerful new negotiating technique: **how can I make this thing work for me?** If you are going to want to harness this powerful tool, then you're going to have to understand why it works.

The main driver behind this technique is that the other side of the table already has **a significant investment** in making the deal happen. The escalation to authority is based on the other side being willing to do more in order to achieve what they think is already almost theirs.

When they encounter the escalating authority tactic, the other side believes that they have only **two choices**. The first is to make a concession and allow the deal to happen. The other is to refuse to make a concession and be willing to sit down and start the negotiating process all over again.

How Can You Defend Against Escalating Authority?

If there's a powerful negotiating tactic out there, then you know that someday **it's going to be used against you**. When this happens, and it will, you'll need to know what to do in order to counteract its powerful force.

Right off the bat, you've got the most powerful countermeasure available to you: leave. **Get up and walk out the door**. If you do this, then all of the power associated with the escalating authority tactic instantly vanishes.

When this tactic starts to be used against you, you need to immediately **inform the rest of your company what is going on**. Your purpose for doing this is pretty simple: you want them to get used to the idea of waiting – no deal is going to be struck anytime soon.

One final countermeasure is to **just wait**. Just as you have a large investment in making a deal happen, so too does the other side of the table. This means that if you just put a stop to everything, they'll soon start to feel as though the deal that was almost theirs is starting to slip away. This may force them to drop their request for more concessions.

What All Of This Means For You

In the end, the use of escalating authority should be viewed simply as being **yet another negotiating tactic** that we all have available to us. As with all such tactics the key is to understand when it should be used.

When you've gotten the other side to commit to a doing a deal, but you think that you can still get some more concessions out of them, the escalation tactic can be **a good tool to use**. However, if someone starts to use it against you, then you'll need to inform the rest of your company so that they will support you as you deal with it.

Anytime other people get involved in a negotiation in which a deal has already been reached **an element of danger is introduced**. The deal that seemed to be so close, may now look farther away. Careful how you use escalating authority – just make sure that the gains that you're looking for are worth the risk that you'll be introducing.

Chapter 5

Why A Missing Person May Be A Negotiator's Best Friend

Chapter 5: Why A Missing Person May Be A Negotiator's Best Friend

Is it possible that **a person who is not present at a negotiation** could be the one person who controls how the negotiation turns out? The answer, somewhat surprisingly, turns out to be an unequivocal yes! If you want to make this negotiating technique work for you (and learn how to defend against it), we're going to have to have a talk...

What Is The Missing Person Authority Tactic?

In order for a sales negotiation to wrap up, you always need a person on your side of the table to approve the final deal. Once you've got all of the details worked out, the final step in the process is for the deal to be presented to this person in order **to get their stamp of approval**.

The missing person tactic occurs when after all of the negotiations have wrapped up, this very important person is **nowhere to be found**. If they can't be found, they can't sign off on the deal that has been reached. This means that things go into a weird sort of suspended animation while everyone waits for that person to reappear.

How Can You Use A Missing Person To Your Advantage?

The power associated with this tactic comes from the simple fact that all that waiting can play havoc with the other side of the table. As the days slip away, the simple fact that they are so tantalizingly close to having a completed deal **starts to eat at them**.

Soon they start to become **desperate to close the deal**. As they search for ways to move things to a close, they start to offer to make additional concessions. Perhaps small concessions in the beginning, but these can become much larger offers as time moves on. Although they are giving something up by making these offers, they view it as a last ditch effort to salvage a deal that seems to be slipping away.

The secret to the missing person tactic is that more often than not, the person with final approval authority **really isn't missing**. Instead they just didn't want to sign the deal as it originally stood. By making themselves "unavailable" they were able to ratchet up the pressure on the other side of the table and improve the quality of the deal that was finally presented to them.

How Can You Defend Against The Missing Person Tactic?

Hopefully you can see how powerful the missing person tactic can be. This does bring up the awkward question about what you should do if you find yourself in a situation where this tactic is **being used against you**.

Clearly you can't stop someone from employing the missing person tactic against you; however, you can **change how you and your firm react to it**. The reason that this tactic is so successful is that it uses time to cause you to do things that you normally would not do.

When you find yourself being subjected to this tactic, the #1 thing that you need to do, and do quickly, is to let everyone at your company understand what is happening. You need to let them know that the negotiations have gone into a sort of **"hold mode"** and that they will remain there until the other side of the table decides to move things forward.

Your best defense is to **do nothing**. By not allowing the passage of time to get to you, you'll take away the power that this tactic gives to the other side of the table. Eventually they'll have to either make the missing person available to approve the deal or they'll have to come back to the table and open up negotiations once again.

What All Of This Means For You

The world of negotiating is filled with different ways to bend the other side of the table to your way of thinking. The missing person tactic is **a classic way** of doing this.

By ensuring that a person who is required to approve any deal that is made becomes **"unavailable"**, you have the ability to put pressure on the other side of the table. As time drags on they'll become more and more desperate to close the deal. This is when they will start to make more concessions just to wrap things up. You need to be careful to not fall into the same trap when this tactic is applied to you.

Time is a constant factor in any sales negotiation. Using the missing person tactic allows you to **harness the power of time** and make it work for you. As with all tactics, you need to be careful when and how you use this approach. Done wisely the missing person tactic may turn out to be the most important member of your negotiating team!

Chapter 6

Sales Negotiators Ask "Do You See What I See…"?

Chapter 6: Sales Negotiators Ask "Do You See What I See..."?

The goal of any negotiation is to get the other side of the table to **see things your way**. Hmm, how are we going to make that happen? What you are going to have to do is to become skilled at finding ways to support the position that you are taking. In order to get better at doing this, I've got 5 tips that will boost your skills...

Tips For Reaching A Deal Faster

If you want to be able to reach a deal with the other side of the table faster, then you're going to have to take the time to give some thought to what it's going to take in order to get them to see things your way. In other words, **you've got some persuading to do**. Here's how to make that happen:

- **It's Only Good If It's Hard:** Call it human nature, call it what you will – for some odd reason, we all seem to want those things that are hard to get. This means that in a negotiation you need to make them see why you want that one thing more than anything else if you are going to be able to reach a deal.

- **Our Ears Don't Work When We're Mad:** I'm pretty sure that those of you with teenagers will fully understand this one. When we become angry during a negotiation, our ears stop working. This means that mad people will reject your message even if what you are offering to them is actually in their best interest.

- **Come Prepared:** It's pretty amazing at just how easily our minds can go blank when we sit down at the negotiating table. That's why it's always a good idea to take the time to write down all of the arguments that you can think of in favor of your positions before you sit down at the negotiating table.

- **The Turtle Won The Race:** I'd like to say that your brilliant words or clearly stated position will convince the other side to see things your way. However, all too often this is not true. What causes the other side to come around to your way of thinking is simply time – lots of it. Be patient and keep restating your main points and eventually the other side of the table will see things your way.

- **Rank Matters:** I'd like to say that one's title doesn't matter during a negotiation; however, that wouldn't be correct. It turns out that the higher that somebody's position is in the company, the less inclined the other side of the table is going to be to argue with him or her.

What All Of This Means For You

Every negotiation has the same goal in mind: finding a way for all parties involved to **reach a successful deal**. The challenge comes from finding a way to get from where everyone starts out to agreeing on that deal in the end.

Skilled negotiators know that they need find ways to **support their position** if they want to have any hope of reaching a deal in a reasonable amount of time. In order to make this happen, you can use the 5 tips that we've discussed in order to steer the other side of the table towards the deal that you want to strike. Try them out and you'll be amazed at how much quicker you're able to wrap-up your next negotiating session!

Chapter 7

The Ultimate Sales Negotiating Goal: A Shared Vision

Chapter 7: The Ultimate Sales Negotiating Goal: A Shared Vision

The goal of any negotiation is to get the other side of the table to **see things your way**. Hmm, how are we going to make that happen? What you are going to have to do is to become skilled at finding ways to support the position that you are taking. In order to get better at doing this, I've got 5 tips that will boost your skills...

Tips For Reaching A Deal Faster

If you want to be able to reach a deal with the other side of the table faster, then you're going to have to take the time to give some thought to what it's going to take in order to get them to see things your way. In other words, **you've got some persuading to do**. Here's how to make that happen:

- **No, You Go First:** Often during a negation you'll find yourself in a situation where you need to communicate two different messages to the other side of the table at the same time. This could be something along the lines of yes we have what you are looking for in the quantity that you need, but the price is going to be higher than you want to pay. In these situations, you need to send the positive message first ("we have what you want") before you send the negative message ("the price is going to be higher than you wanted").

- **Focus On What They Want:** A negotiation can take a great deal of both time and energy. If you want to boost your chances of finally reaching an agreement with the other side, then you need to keep stressing just how great it's going to be when both sides are able to finally reach an agreement. Keeping the focus on the benefit of the deal is what will make reaching an agreement that much easier.

- **I Remember Promises:** Professional negotiators know that if you are able to understand what the other side of the table really wants and deliver to them a message that generates a need in them, then when you provide them with information about how to meet that need, they'll remember what you've said. However, there is a danger here. If the message that you deliver about their need is filled with threats about what could happen, then the other side will shut down and will reject your proposed solution.

- **Lack Of Involvement Is More Believable:** Negotiations can get bogged down as each side tries to convince the other side to see things their way. When this happens, it can be helpful to have someone who has not been involved in the negotiations swoop in and deliver the same message that you've been trying to get across. Simply by having a non-involved person show up can often make the message more believable.

- **Obscure Other Opinions:** I know that during a negotiation, my heart will drop into my shoes if the other side learns that some important person has decided that they oppose something that I am trying to convince them to do. Because of these experiences, I now try to isolate the other side during the negotiations so that outside opinions won't complicate the negotiations.

What All Of This Means For You

Every negotiation has the same goal in mind: finding a way for all parties involved to **reach a successful deal**. The challenge comes from finding a way to get from where everyone starts out to agreeing on that deal in the end.

Skilled negotiators know that they need find ways to **support their position** if they want to have any hope of reaching a deal in a reasonable amount of time. In order to make this happen, you can use the 5 tips that we've discussed in order to steer the other side of the table towards the deal that you want to strike. Try them out and you'll be amazed at how much quicker you're able to wrap-up your next negotiating session!

Chapter 8

I've Met The Negotiating Devil And He Lives In the Details

Chapter 8: I've Met The Negotiating Devil And He Lives In the Details

You can trust the other side of the table when you are negotiating with them, right? I mean sure, we'll all try to get a leg up during the negotiations and use as many negotiation styles and negotiating techniques as we possibly can in order to get the best deal, but once the negotiation process is over everything will be cool, right? As wise men have said, **it's not over until it's over** and this counts double for a sales negotiation...

Can You Say Fine Print?

When we say that we are trying to **reach a deal** when we engage in a sales negotiation, what are we really talking about? Is it that we're trying to get to that moment at the negotiating table where you look into the eyes of the other side and say "I think that I can live with that" and then you both shake hands?

The answer is, of course, no. The deal that was negotiated with the other side of the table is **the one that is written down**. The negotiation definition says that all that counts are the words that are put on the paper that finally gets signed by both sides – not the discussions that we had during the negotiations.

That's why so many negotiators can get tripped up when they don't do the final step in a negotiation: **reviewing the draft written proposal** in order to make sure that it accurately reflects what the negotiators agreed to.

It is far too easy for negotiators to leave **"the details"** to the legal or contracts team to finalize. However, since they may not have been involved in the actual negotiators, they may not fully understand what the two sides agreed to.

Additionally, the written document provides the other side of the table with the perfect opportunity to **claw back some of the concessions that they made** during their negotiations with you. If they offer to use a boilerplate document to create the final agreement, be very careful. Their boilerplate may contain a lot of words that create a better deal for them than for you.

How To Get The Devil Out Of Your Details

The worst kind of surprise is the one that you get when a deal is being executed and **something happens that you didn't expect**. A payment is late, a delivery doesn't arrive, or a price is higher than you expected. When you go to complain to the other side, they point out that what they've done is covered by the contract that you signed.

When you check the contract, it turns out that they are correct. What happened is that there was **a detail buried somewhere deep in the back pages** of the contract that gave the other side the ability to do what they are doing.

In order to prevent this from happening, you know what you need to do. You need to make sure that **you have plenty of time** to sit down and carefully go over the entire draft contract from front to back before you sign it. Using a standardized checklist can help.

In fact, since you are not perfect, you really need to make sure that **you get others to take a look at the draft contract**. You know what they say about having many eyes look at something...

The most effective technique that I have used to get the devil out of the details of any agreement that you are going to be signing is also the most tiring. This is when you **get a group of people together in a room** and you all review the draft contract at the same time line-by-line.

As painful and time consuming as this type of review is, I've found it to be the most effective. The presence of so many people looking at the same document means that there is **less chance** that something is going to slip past you and come back to bite you later on.

What All Of This Means For You

When we are conducting a principled negotiation with the other side of the table, our guard is up – we're watching to see what negotiating trick they might pull next. Once a deal has been reached, **we tend to let our guard down** – it's all over now.

It turns out that we might be doing this too quickly. The ultimate deal that is reached is going to be **documented in the paperwork that gets signed**. If the other side tucks some items in there that can work against us, signing the deal could turn out to be a costly mistake. Take the time to read any deal very closely before you sign it!

Human nature being what it is, we like to gear up for a confrontation (negotiation) and then ramp back down once we think that the event is over. The clever negotiator realizes that **it's not over until it's over** and waits until the ink is dry on the signed deal before he or she lets their guard down.

Chapter 9

When "Yes" Means "No" And What To Do About It

Chapter 9: When "Yes" Means "No" And What To Do About It

What is the goal of any negotiation? The negotiation definition says that the ultimate goal is simply to reach a deal with the other side. Ah ha! Now this is where things start to really get interesting – after you've sorted through all of the negotiation styles and negotiating techniques that both sides have used, **how can you tell when you've reached a deal with the other side?** Could it be when they have said "yes" to your offer of a deal? You might think that this is the case, but be careful – sometimes "yes" can really mean "no"…!

When An Acceptance Is Not An Acceptance

Negotiations requires great deal of work. When you move through the negotiation process and get close to striking a deal with the other side of the table, you may start to **feel that sense of relief** that things are just about done. However, that's not always the case.

What may happen is that you believe that you've negotiated a deal with the other side of the table that both sides can live with. They tell you that they need to take the deal to the final approval authority on their side to get their blessing. They assure you that **this should be no big deal**.

That's when the clock starts running. The other side goes away and **you don't hear back anything from them**. Perhaps you reach out to them and ask for a status update. They assure you that everything is still on track and there is just some minor issue (people on vacation, etc.) that is holding things up.

Time drags on. You might check with them a few more times and the answer that you get back is always the same – **there is no problem**, the deal is going to be approved. However, what finally happens is that the deal comes back to you with a rejection note. The reason can be almost anything, but the simple fact is that the deal that you thought that you had in hand just isn't going to happen.

What has happened here is that **you've been had**. The other side used the deal that you had negotiated with them as a bargaining chip in some other deal that they were working on. You were identified as their fallback position if the parties involved in the other deal couldn't reach a compromise. Clearly this other party gave in, a deal was struck and now the deal that you thought was going to happen for you isn't going to happen.

How To Deal With A "Yes" That Really Is A "No"

The reason that you can get caught (and used) in one of these yes / no deals is because **there are too many people involved**. With so many different people being involved, the possibility of faulty information getting back to you is increased.

In order to prevent yourself from getting caught up in this type of situation, **you need to step up and take charge**. Another way of saying this is that you've got to find ways to cut out the middle man.

Insist on **dealing directly** with the decision making principles who are involved in the deal. Get rid of the brokers and middlemen that may have their own agendas that conflict with what you are trying to accomplish.

Finally, take on some of the administrative tasks that every negotiation session has associated with itself. One way that the middlemen can buy themselves time is to inform you that **various administrative tasks are taking longer than they should**. Eliminate this possibility by doing those tasks yourself.

What All Of This Means For You

In order to wrap up a negotiation, you need to get the other side of the table **to agree to the deal that has been proposed**. That's all well and good, but sometimes when they say "yes", they really mean "no" – clearly they aren't practicing principled negotiation.

The reasons for this confusing state of affairs can be many. Most common is the one in which the deal that you've brokered with the other side **is being used as a powerful tool** to get some other party to agree to terms that the other side is trying to impose on them. Your deal will never be accepted – you are just being used. You can prevent this from happening to you by taking matters into your own hands and eliminating the middle men who could feed you the false information. Deal directly with the deal makers and you'll have a better chance of knowing what the real deal is.

Trust is a key part of any negotiation. You can't always ensure that the other side is negotiating with a good intent, but you can take steps to make sure that if they have any plans of saying "yes" when they really mean "no, that you get to say "no" to those plans first!

Chapter 10

Negotiators Know How To Get A Deal Into Shape

Chapter 10: Negotiators Know How To Get A Deal Into Shape

So there you are, you've just presented what you think should be an acceptable deal to the other side of the table and yet it doesn't look like they are going to go for it. What gives? Experienced negotiators know that sometimes during negotiations the other side of the table can be made to agree to a deal if only you know how to **change the shape of the deal** that you are proposing to them…

What's Wrong With Your Proposal?

How a proposal looks to you may not be the same way that it looks to the other side of the table – this has nothing to do with negotiation styles or negotiating techniques and everything to do with what is being negotiated. One reason for this is that **you have a particular timeframe** that you are thinking about when you consider this deal; however, that timeline may not match the way that the other side of the table sees the world.

If you were able to reach an agreement with the other side, then you might want to jump in and get the deal moving quickly. They, on the other hand, might be thinking about all of the other things that they have going on and they might want to **take things slower**.

When the other side has a different schedule than you do, your ability to reach a deal with them is **put at risk**. The good news is that experienced negotiators realize this and are able to adapt their proposal to resolve this issue.

How Do You Change The Shape Of A Deal?

When the timeline of a deal is causing the other side of the table to hesitate in agreeing to it, it becomes your responsibility to take control of the negotiation process and **change the proposal's "time shape"**. What this means is that you'll make changes to when and even perhaps how a deal will get done. This could be as simple as either making it so that all of the work happens quickly after the deal is agreed to or that it happens slowly over time.

One thing that every negotiator needs to realize is that any time that you propose a change to the time shape of a deal, the other side has to sit up and **pay attention**. Your changes will modify the risk / reward characteristics of the deal and they need to evaluate if it has suddenly become a better (or worse) deal for them.

Keep in mind that how long it takes to do a job is only one of the many deal characteristics that can be changed. You can also **modify the sequence** in which the work is done. Making either of these types of changes can turn a deadlocked negotiation into a successful deal.

What Does All Of This Mean For You?

When the other side of the table is considering a proposal that you've made to them, they may be **rejecting it for the wrong reasons**. They may have no problem with what you are proposing; it's the shape of the deal that might be putting them off. There's nothing in the negotiation definition that will tell you how to deal with this kind of situation.

What this mean for you as a negotiator is that you need to get clever at **changing the shape of your deal**. This may have something to do with when the work gets done. Changing the time shape of when the deal is performed can completely change how the other side of the table looks at the deal. Good news – this all fits within what we consider to be a principled negotiation.

Experienced negotiators know that once the other side of the table becomes interested in your proposal, the next step is for you to make sure that the shape of the deal meets their needs. Play around with when the work gets done and you just might find yourself with a signed contract!

Chapter 11

Successful Negotiators Know What Money Looks Like

Chapter 11: Successful Negotiators Know What Money Looks Like

In the end, just about every negotiation comes down to one thing: **money**. You would think that we could all agree on just exactly what this thing that we call money looks like, but there you would be wrong. Forget everything that you've learned about different negotiation styles and negotiating techniques. Instead for just a moment, focus on the money — it turns out that money has a shape, and this shape might be what is keeping us from reaching a deal with the other side of the table during negotiations. Let's talk about how we can change the shape of money...

The Time Shape Of Money

So just exactly what is this **"time shape of money"** thing? It's actually pretty simple. One side of the table has the money, and the other side wants to get their hands on it. That money can be paid in a number of different ways and those payments can even be delayed.

As a negotiator you need to understand that different parties have different perspectives on the cash that is being discussed as a part of the negotiation. You'd be amazed at the number of times that I've been involved in a negotiation and although I had assumed that the other side of the table was flush with cash, for one reason or another they were **almost desperate to get their hands on the cash** that we were talking about as quickly as possible!

As a negotiator you need to understand that as part of the negotiation process, the way that that the cash is shaped may play a big role in how the other side of the table is looking at any deal that you are trying to put together. What this means is that you are going to have to take the time to explore how you can **make the time shape of money work for you**. You may end up being able to create a better deal for yourself simply by reshaping the price.

How You Can Make The Time Shape Of Money Work For You In A Negotiation

If you can agree with me that the shape of the money involved in a deal that is being negotiated may be a critical factor in your ability to create a deal that works for both sides of the table, then we need to understand how to go about making this happen. **It's all about time**.

When money is a part of a negotiation, we need to keep in mind that money can be **paid in a wide variety of different ways**. The other side of the table may be eager to receive most if not all of the money up front – they want to get their hands on it as soon as possible. In other cases, they may be looking for a much longer payment period.

Things that you and I might believe should be fixed, such as **monthly payments**, may actually be something that the other side is hoping to make variable for whatever reason. The length of time that the payments will be made is another factor that you can control: some parties will want the period to be long while others will be looking for a much shorter period.

Just to keep things interesting, you must not always assume that the other side wants to be paid! In certain cases, the other side may want the payments to be **sent to some other party**. There can be a wide variety of reasons for this; however, I've often found that tax considerations can play a big role in such decisions.

What All Of This Means For You

All money is not created equal. Well, that's not really true – money is money, but what negotiators need to realize is part of the negotiation definition tells us that all money comes with a time shape associated with it. If you can learn how to change the shape of the money that is part of your negotiation, then you'll have a powerful new tool.

The other side of the table sees the money that is part of the negotiations in a particular way – **it has a specific shape**. The money might be coming to them up front, or it might be coming slowly over time. They may not want it to come this way and that's where you can step in and change the shape of the money being negotiated.

Knowing that money has a shape is a key realization for negotiators. The next skill that they have to have is to be able to make the changes that will transform the shape of the money that is part of this principled negotiation. By doing this you just may be able to change a negotiation that seems to be going nowhere into one that creates a deal that both sides of the table can live with.

Chapter 12

When Is It Time To Bring In The Mediator?

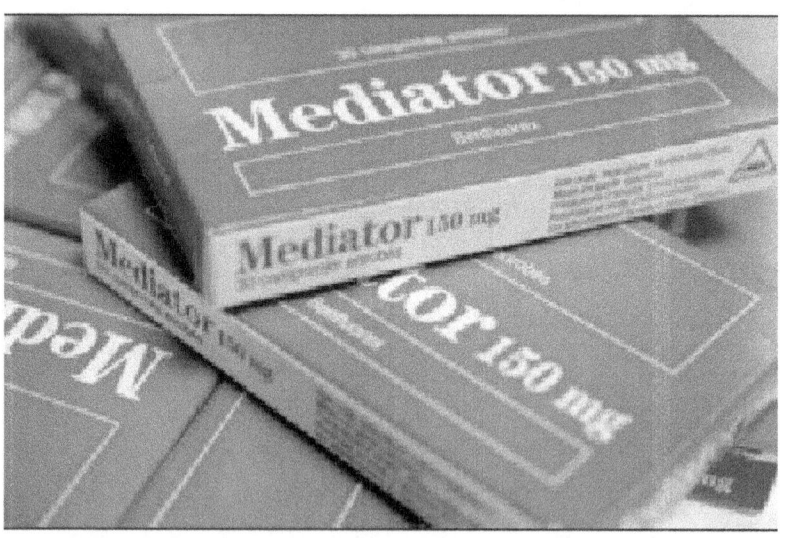

Chapter 12: When Is It Time To Bring In The Mediator?

I'd like to be able to tell you that there is nothing in this world that two negotiators can't work out between themselves. I said that I'd like to be able to tell you this, but I can't because it's not true. The sad truth of the matter is that in certain circumstances, maybe it because of our different negotiation styles or negotiating techniques, we are just not able to see eye-to-eye with the other side of the table. When this happens, **it may be time to bring in a mediator...**

What Does A Mediator Do?

Mediators play two different roles in a negotiation. The first occurs during the actual negotiations themselves. A mediator can be brought in to **bring together** two sides who for whatever reason because of what is being negotiated may not be able to come together without some outside help. The other role that they play occurs after the deal is done.

Negotiations consist of many different phases. During the implementation phase of a negotiation, after the deal has been signed and both parties are supposed to be working to make it happen, a mediator may be needed if one or more parties **doesn't think that the terms of the agreement are being lived up to**. This happens so often that it really should be part of the negotiation definition.

The role that a mediator plays is to find a way to **harmonize the differing viewpoints** that are held by each side of the negotiation. The reason that you would bring in a mediator is because the alternative is much messier – you'd have to take the other side to court.

How Do Mediators Help A Negotiation?

You may be asking yourself, so **just exactly what do mediators do?** That's actually a very good question that does not have one specific answer. Instead, it runs out that mediators do a number of different things during the negotiation process depending on the situation that they find themselves in. Here are a few of the things that you could expect a mediator to do:

New Ideas: Pitch new ideas to each side of the negotiations. It turns out that each side may be more open to hearing about a new idea from a mediator than if the other party in the negotiation made the proposal for the new idea.

Realistic Suggestions: A mediator can help both sides to suggest what are considered to be realistic suggestions.

Come Back: Walking out of a negotiation is a fairly common tactic. However, after this has been done, it can be difficult to determine when you can return to the negotiating table. A mediator can be the person who invites you to return to the table.

Not Get Angry: a mediator can take the time to listen to what both sides of the table want in terms of some controversial topic without becoming angry or upset. Once the idea has been expressed the mediator can have an unemotional discussion with you about your position.

Compromise: a mediator can make suggestions to either side for ways that they can compromise in order to keep the discussions moving on without appearing to be weak.

What Does All Of This Mean For You?

As negotiators, we like to think that we can solve just about any situation. The reality is that sometimes we are not able to communicate clearly with the other side for a whole variety of different reasons. When this happens, **it may be time to bring in a mediator**.

A mediator **serves as a go-between** for the different negotiating parties. A mediator has the ability to help out both during the principled negotiation itself and afterwards during the implementation phase. Mediators accomplish their task by selling new ideas to both sides, listening, and showing where compromises can be made.

The ultimate goal of any negotiation is to **reach a deal with the other side**. Sometimes this can be just too difficult to do by ourselves. When we hit a wall and are not able to either start a negotiation or continue one, it may be time to bring in a mediator. If we judge the success of a negotiation by the deal that gets created, then using a mediator may just be what it takes to get us to where we want to be.

It's from the forge of failure that the steel of success is formed.

Hard Work Does Not Guarantee Success, But Success Does Not Happen Without Hard Work.

- Dr. Jim Anderson

Create An Effective Negotiating Team At Your Company!

Dr. Jim Anderson is available to provide training and coaching on the topics that are the most important to people who have to negotiate: how can my team effectively prepare for and execute a successful negotiation that will get us what we both want and need?

Dr. Anderson believes that in order to both learn and remember what he says, audiences need to laugh. Each one of his speeches is full of fun and humor so that what he says "sticks" with everyone.

Dr. Anderson's Negotiating Training Includes:

1. How to plan for a negotiation: what information do you need and where can you find it?

2. What's the best way to explore how a deal can be created during a negotiation?

3. How can you bring a negotiation to a close without giving in to the other side?

Dr. Jim Anderson works with over 100 customers per year. To invite Dr. Anderson to work with you, contact him at:

Phone: 813-418-6970 or
Email: jim@BlueElephantConsulting.com

Photo Credits:

Cover – lovecatz

https://www.flickr.com/photos/lovecatz/

Chapter 1 - Paul Townsend

https://www.flickr.com/photos/brizzlebornandbred/

Chapter 2 - Like_the_Grand_Canyon

https://www.flickr.com/photos/like_the_grand_canyon/

Chapter 3 - the666 project666

http://www.the666.com/eng518.htm

Chapter 4 - Ricardo Diaz

https://www.flickr.com/photos/ricardodiaz/

Chapter 5 - Jacob Freeze

https://www.flickr.com/photos/37773726@N08/

Chapter 6 - Lennart Takanen

https://www.flickr.com/photos/takanen/

Chapter 7 - 酷哥哥

https://www.flickr.com/photos/khooyu/

Chapter 8 - Andrea Kirkby

https://www.flickr.com/photos/andreakirkby/

Chapter 9 - Naked Faris

https://www.flickr.com/photos/nakedfaris/

Chapter 10 - Fit Approach

https://www.flickr.com/photos/fitapproach/

Chapter 11 - AJC1

https://www.flickr.com/photos/ajc1/

Chapter 12 - DES Daughter

https://www.flickr.com/photos/diethylstilbestrol/

Other Books By The Author

Product Management

Manage Your Customers, Manage Your Product: Techniques For Product Managers To Better Understand What Their Customers Really Want

How Product Managers Can Sell More Of Their Product: Tips & Techniques For Product Managers To Better Understand How To Sell Their Product

How Product Managers Can Sell More Of Their Product: Tips & Techniques For Product Managers To Better Understand How To Sell Their Product

How To Create A Successful Product That Customers Will Want: Techniques For Product Managers To Boost Product Sales And Increase Customer Satisfaction

What Product Managers Need To Know About World-Class Product Development: How Product Managers Can Create Successful Products

How Product Managers Can Learn To Understand Their Customers: Techniques For Product Managers To

Better Understand What Their Customers Really Want

Product Management Secrets: Techniques For Product Managers To Boost Product Sales And Increase Customer Satisfaction

Product Development Lessons For Product Managers: How Product Managers Can Create Successful Products

Customer Lessons For Product Managers: Techniques For Product Managers To Better Understand What Their Customers Really Want

Product Failure Lessons For Product Managers: Examples Of Products That Have Failed For Product Managers To Learn From

Communication Skills For Product Managers: The Communication Skills That Product Managers Need To Know How To Use In Order To Have A Successful Product

How To Have A Successful Product Manager Career: The Things That You Need To Be Doing TODAY In Order To Have A Successful Product Manager Career

Product Manager Product Success: How to keep your product on track and make it become a success

Public Speaking

How To Get Ready To Give The Perfect Speech: What Tools To Use To Create Your Next Speech So That Your Message Will Be Remembered Forever!

Creating Speeches That Work: How To Create A Speech That Will Make Your Message Be Remembered Forever!

How To Organize A Speech In Order To Make Your Point: How to put together a speech that will capture and hold your audience's attention

Changing How You Speak To Overcome Your Fear Of Speaking: Change techniques that will transform a speech into a memorable event

Delivering Excellence: How To Give Presentations That Make A Difference: Presentation techniques that will transform a speech into a memorable event

Tools Speakers Need In Order To Give The Perfect Speech: What tools to use to create your next speech so that your message will be remembered forever!

How To Create A Speech That Will Be Remembered

Secrets To Organizing A Speech For Maximum Impact: How to put together a speech that will capture and hold your audience's attention

How To Become A Better Speaker By Changing How You Speak: Change techniques that will transform a speech into a memorable event

How To Give A Great Presentation: Presentation techniques that will transform a speech into a memorable event

How To Rehearse In Order To Give The Perfect Speech: How to effectively rehearse your next speech to that your message be remembered forever!

Secrets To Creating The Perfect Speech: How to create a speech that will make your message be remembered forever!

Secrets To Organizing The Perfect Speech: How to organize the best speech of your life!

Secrets To Planning The Perfect Speech: How to plan to give the best speech of your life

How To Show What You Mean During A Presentation: How to use visual techniques to transform a speech into a memorable event

CIO Skills

How CIOs Can Take Their Career To The Next Level: How CIOs Can Work With The Entire Company In Order To Be Successful

How CIOs Can Bring Business And IT Together: How CIOs Can Use Their Technical Skills To Help Their Company Solve Real-World Business Problems

New IT Technology Issues Facing CIOs: How CIOs Can Stay On Top Of The Changes In The Technology That Powers The Company

Keeping The Barbarians Out: How CIOs Can Secure Their Department and Company: Tips And Techniques For CIOs To Use In Order To Secure Both Their IT Department And Their Company

What CIOs Need To Know In Order To Successfully Manage An IT Department: Decision Making Skills That Every CIO Needs To Have In Order To Be Able To Make The Right Choices

Becoming A Powerful And Effective Leader: Tips And Techniques That IT Managers Can Use In Order To

Develop Leadership Skills

CIO Secrets For Growing Innovation: Tips And Techniques For CIOs To Use In Order To Make Innovation Happen In Their IT Department

Your Success As A CIO Depends On How Well You Communicate: Tips And Techniques For CIOs To Use In Order To Become Better Communicators

What CIOs Need To Know About Working With Partners: Techniques For CIOs To Use In Order To Be Able To Successfully Work With Partners

Critical CIO Management Skills: Decision Making Skills That Every CIO Needs To Have In Order To Be Able To Make The Right Choices

How CIOs Can Make Innovation Happen: Tips And Techniques For CIOs To Use In Order To Make Innovation Happen In Their IT Department

CIO Communication Skills Secrets: Tips And Techniques For CIOs To Use In Order To Become Better Communicators

Managing Your CIO Career: Steps That CIOs Have To Take In Order To Have A Long And Successful Career

CIO Business Skills: How CIOs can work effectively with the rest of the company!

IT Manager Skills

Understanding What Leadership Means For IT Managers: Tips And Techniques That IT Managers Can Use In Order To Develop Leadership Skills

How IT Managers Can Use New Technology To Meet Today's IT Challenges: Technologies That IT Managers Can Use In Order to Make Their Teams More Productive

How To Build High Performance IT Teams: Tips And Techniques That IT Managers Can Use In Order To Develop Productive Teams

Save Yourself, Save Your Job – How To Manage Your IT Career: Secrets That IT Managers Can Use In Order To Have A Successful Career

Growing Your CIO Career: How CIOs Can Work With The Entire Company In Order To Be Successful

How IT Managers Can Make Innovation Happen: Tips And Techniques For IT Managers To Use In Order To Make Innovation Happen In Their Teams

Staffing Skills IT Managers Must Have: Tips And Techniques That IT Managers Can Use In Order To Correctly Staff Their Teams

Secrets Of Effective Leadership For IT Managers: Tips And Techniques That IT Managers Can Use In Order To Develop Leadership Skills

IT Manager Career Secrets: Tips And Techniques That IT Managers Can Use In Order To Have A Successful Career

IT Manager Budgeting Skills: How IT Managers Can Request, Manage, Use, And Track Their Funding

Secrets Of Managing Budgets: What IT Managers Need To Know In Order To Understand How Their Company Uses Money

Negotiating

The Art Of Packaging A Negotiation: How To Develop The Skill Of Assembling Potential Trades In Order To Get The Best Possible Outcome

Getting What You Want In A Negotiation By Learning How To Signal: How To Develop The Skill Of Effective Signaling In A Negotiation In Order To Get The Best Possible Outcome

Exploring How To Get The Deal That You Want In A Negotiation: How To Develop The Skill Of Exploring What Is Possible In A Negotiation In Order To Reach The Best Possible Deal

Use The Power Of Arguing To Win Your Next Negotiation: How To Develop The Skill Of Effective Arguing In A Negotiation In Order To Get The Best Possible Outcome

Learn How To Signal In Your Next Negotiation: How To Develop The Skill Of Effective Signaling In A Negotiation In Order To Get The Best Possible Outcome

Learn The Skill Of Exploring In A Negotiation: How To Develop The Skill Of Exploring What Is Possible In A Negotiation In Order To Reach The Best Possible Deal

Learn How To Argue In Your Next Negotiation: How To Develop The Skill Of Effective Arguing In A Negotiation In Order To Get The Best Possible Outcome|

How To Open Your Next Negotiation: How To Start A Negotiation In Order To Get The Best Possible

Outcome

Preparing For Your Next Negotiation: What You Need To Do BEFORE A Negotiation Starts In Order To Get The Best Possible Deal

Learn How To Package Trades In Your Next Negotiation

All Good Things Come To An End: How To Close A Negotiation - How To Develop The Skill Of Closing In Order To Get The Best Possible Outcome From A Negotiation

Take No Prisoners In Your Next Negotiation: How To Start A Negotiation In Order To Get The Best Possible Outcome

Miscellaneous

How To Heal A Broken Leg – Fast!: Understanding how to deal with a broken leg in order to start walking again quickly

How Software Defined Networking (SDN) Is Going To Change Your World Forever: The Revolution In Network Design And How It Affects You

The Power Of Virtualization: How It Affects Memory, Servers, and Storage: The Revolution In Creating Virtual Devices And How It Affects You

The Internet-Enabled Successful School District Superintendent: How To Use The Internet To Boost Parental Involvement In Your Schools

Power Distribution Unit (PDU) Secrets: What Everyone Who Works In A Data Center Needs To Know!

Making The Jump: How To Land Your Dream Job When You Get Out Of College!

How To Use The Internet To Create Successful Students And Involved Parents

How To Develop The Skill Of Closing In Order To Get The Best Possible Outcome From A Negotiation

This book has been written with one goal in mind – to show you how to successfully close your next negotiation. It's not easy being a negotiator and so we're going to show you how to successfully close the negotiation in a way that will get you the deal that you want!

Let's Make Your Negotiation A Success!

What You'll Find Inside:

- **QUICK CLOSE NEGOTIATING: 4 WAYS TO GET THERE FASTER**

- **WHAT DOES "TAKE IT OR LEAVE IT" MEAN IN A SALES NEGOTIATION?**

- **THE ULTIMATE SALES NEGOTIATING GOAL: A SHARED VISION**

- **WHEN "YES" MEANS "NO" AND WHAT TO DO ABOUT IT**

Dr. Jim Anderson brings his 25 years of real-world experience to this book. He's been a negotiator at some of the world's largest firms. He's going to show you what you need to do (and not do!) in order to get the best deal out of your next negotiation!

www.ingramcontent.com/pod-product-compliance
Lightning Source LLC
Chambersburg PA
CBHW070212230526
45471CB00002B/932